common
critters

TILBURY HOUSE PUBLISHERS
Thomaston, Maine
www.tilburyhouse.com

Text © 2020 by Pat Brisson
Illustrations © 2020 by Dan Tavis

Library of Congress
Control Number: 2019957044

15 16 17 18 19 20 XXX 10 9 8 7 6 5 4 3 2 1

Designed by Frame25 Productions
Printed and bound in China

common critters

The Wildlife in Your Neighborhood

Poems by Pat Brisson

Illustrated by Dan Tavis

TILBURY HOUSE PUBLISHERS,
THOMASTON, MAINE

Do you like to go exploring?

Do insects interest you?
Are you always on the lookout
for a furry beast or two?

Do you get a bit excited
when you spy a bird nearby?
Do you want to know some things
about some things that crawl or fly?

There are creatures all around you,
not exotic, but not tame.
Though most are pretty common,
they're intriguing just the same.

To see these common critters
you don't need to go too far.
Just take a careful look around—
they're everywhere you are.

Crow

Oh, shiny-black and noisy crow,
you are the loudest bird I know,
gathered with your friends in trees,
cawing harshly on the breeze.

You're not a vegetarian,
for you eat frogs, worms, mice, and carrion.
When you find food, you call your friends—
your cawing never seems to end.

And could this fact be much absurder?
A group of you is called a *murder*!
In winter roosts ten thousand deep,
what you murder is our sleep.

Earthworm

The worm lives safely underground—
moves quite slowly, makes no sound.
In gardens he is highly prized
for keeping soil well-fertilized,

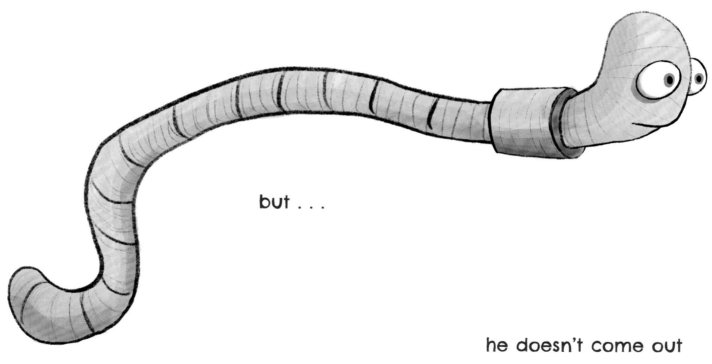

but . . .

he doesn't come out
when birds are about,
for some birds will eat him
if ever they meet him.

Robin

When warmer days begin to dawn,
the robins come back to our lawn.
I see them tug, tug, tugging worms
that stretch and wiggle, pull and squirm.

They need those worms to feed the birds
whose tiny, squealing chirps I heard,
just-hatched from eggshells greenish-blue.
(They'll feed their babies berries, too.)

Those mouths are big, those bodies small,
with feathers barely there at all.
In two weeks they'll be fledgling size,
and soon they'll take off for the skies.

Mourning Dove

This bird's a sign of peace and love,
the pigeon's cousin—mourning dove.
It isn't really sad at all,
but has a saddish-sounding call.

Its feathers are a grayish-brown;
it looks for seeds upon the ground.
It makes its nest up in a tree
and lays an egg or two (not three).

Baby mourning doves are *squabs*,
and feeding is both parents' jobs.
When mourning doves are on their flyways,
they're as fast as cars on highways.

Of all the birds I know and love,
my favorite is the mourning dove.

Garden Slug

Its eyes are found above its head
on feelers long and slender.
It likes to eat the garden plants
that sprout up green and tender.

It looks just like a shell-less snail
but doesn't seem to mind,
and as it slowly glides away,
it leaves a trail behind.

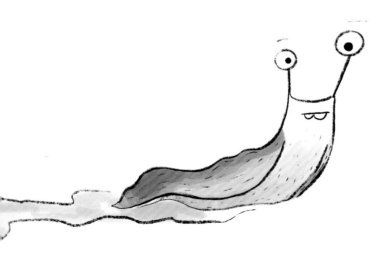

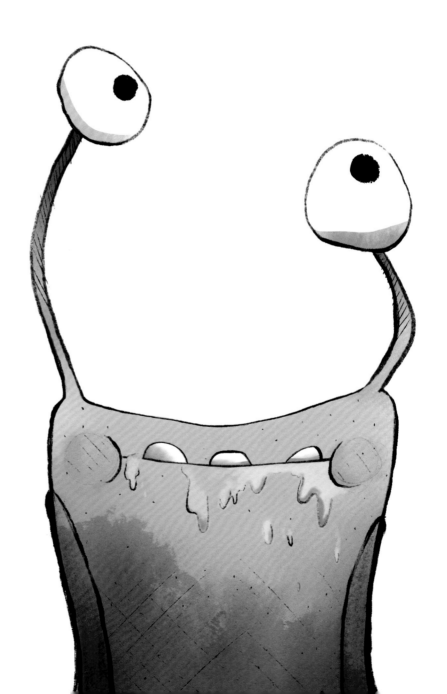

Honeybee

Honeybees fly here and there
buzzing through the sunny air,
on their nectar hunt for hours,
as they search for fresh new flowers.

They take nectar to the hive,
where it keeps their young alive
after it's been turned to honey.
And isn't this fact kind of funny:

Their hive is always Home Sweet Home
because they live in honeycomb!

Ant

Underground their tunnels grow
by their labor sure and slow.
What great excavating skill!
Above the ground a small anthill
indicates that down below
ants are moving to and fro.

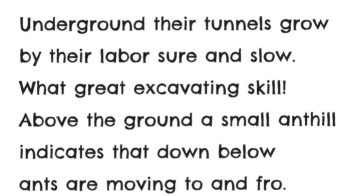

Bit by bit, they bring out soil.
Oh, how hard those small ants toil!
They are strong and work together.
Look for them in sunny weather.
When they're hungry they go find
crumbs you may have left behind.

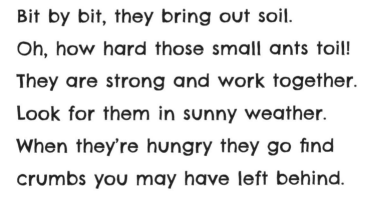

Caterpillar

This chubby little herbivore
likes to eat, then eat some more.
It sheds its skin, then grows another,
but won't look like its dad or mother
until it spends some time marooned
in a chrysalis, or small cocoon.

It follows metamorphic urges
to break out, and what emerges
is a moth or butterfly
that dries its wings and starts to fly.

Cabbage White Butterfly

It's one of the first we see flying in spring,
mostly white with black spots on each wing.
(The tips of each wing look a little, I think,
as though they were dipped in a pot of black ink.)

If you're growing cabbage, you'll think them a pest,
for their caterpillars love cabbage the best.
But once they have had about all they can eat,
their chrysalis grows—this is really a feat!

And after a while what they were disappears,
and what do you know—there are butterflies here!
Each day in the garden they flutter all over,
sipping nectar from asters and clover.

So when hungry green caterpillars crawl on your plants,
think of the butterflies that will soon dance.
If you want those butterflies visiting you,
you have to expect metamorphosis, too.

Ladybug

If you're an aphid, you should know
the ladybug's your mortal foe.
She'll eat you up quite quickly, then
she'll move along and eat your friend.
She looks so cute—black spots on red—
but don't be fooled—you'll end up dead.

Praying Mantis

The praying mantis, still and green,
blends in so well, he's barely seen.
His big head turns—his bulging eyes
are searching for some insect prize.

I know that he's a carnivore
and guess that he is praying for
a bug or two to wander by:
a spider, wasp, or butterfly.

He spots his prey:
a fast attack!
He gobbles down
a housefly snack.

Housefly

A housefly, flying by my head,
stopped and landed on my bread.
My mother gave my dad a shout
to get that pesky housefly "OUT!"

They carry germs, can make you sick,
and poop in what you're eating. Ick!
Though spiders, birds, and frogs adore them,
most people, you will find, abhor them.

The fly is dangerous, though small.
Don't let them in your house at all.

Spider

If you want to be a spider
here is what you need to do:
change the legs that you are wearing—
you'll need eight now, not just two—
and each leg needs seven segments
with three claws on each leg's end.
Put them on a cephalothorax;
that's what I recommend.

Don't forget eight eyes for seeing,
and some fangs on two small jaws,
and remember to add venom—
that will give your victims pause.
The silk that you'll be spinning
comes from spinnerets you'll find
in six glands that are embedded
in your spidery behind.

If you still need more directions
on the spider you should be,
go and ask another spider—
this is all you'll get from me.

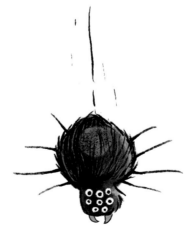

Squirrel

How I wish that I could be
like the squirrel in that tall tree,
climbing branches high and low,
leaping where I want to go;
holding tightly with the claws
on my handy dandy paws;
scampering fast along a wire,
never fearful, going higher;
running straight up trees and then
running straight back down again.

Oh, I wish that I could be
like the squirrel in that tall tree!

Skunk

I very rarely see you,
yet I know that you've been there,
when all around me is a very
pungent skunky air.

It always makes my eyes burn
and it makes me want to cough,
and though I'd like to see you,
you have already run off.

Omnivorous, you're happy
eating insects, snakes, or berries;
you'll even eat our garbage,
though it's not too sanitary.

The great horned owl's not scared of
your evil-smelling spray,
but that spray is good at keeping
other predators away.

Cricket

Under fading summer skies,
crickets chirp their lullabies,
saying, "Go to sleep, my friend,
another day is at its end.

"Tomorrow you can run and play
and look for critters through the day,
but now it's time to close your eyes
and listen to our lullabies."

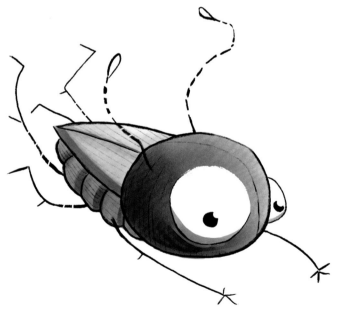

Facts about Common Critters

The illustrator of this book is the first to admit that in the real world, animals don't look the way he has drawn them. For example, a caterpillar doesn't have big front teeth, a garden slug doesn't have big goggly eyes on its feelers, and an earthworm doesn't have eyes at all. But Dan Tavis decided to have some fun with his illustrations; he decided to exercise a little *artistic license* to help them tell stories.

If you've seen the Ice Age animated movies, you already know about artistic license. It's the artist's version of poetic license, which Pat Brisson talks about below in "A Peek into the Poet's Toolkit." If you want to see what one of these animals *really* looks like, just type it into a search engine. You'll find all sorts of photos. After all, these are not just critters—they're *common* critters!

Crow

Because crows can make and use tools, they are considered to be among the world's smartest animals. They also recognize and remember human faces.

Crows can mimic the sounds of other animals and change their calls to communicate warnings, threats, cheers, and other messages. The warnings are heeded not just by fellow crows, but by other animals as well.

Crows build their nest an average of 24 feet above the ground and prefer to nest in evergreens. They will eat whatever food is available and often travel up to 40 miles in a day to find food.

Earthworm

If an earthworm is cut in two, the front end can regenerate (grow into a complete earthworm) if more than half of it is still intact. The tail end will die.

Earthworms can live six years or more but will die if they freeze. In the winter, they burrow about 6 feet into the ground and stay there until the weather turns warmer.

Earthworms help bring nutrients from deep in the soil to the surface. They also help aerate, or break up, the soil, which helps plants to grow.

Real-life earthworms don't have eyes, though they can sense changes in light intensity. The raised band, or *clitellum*, is where eggs are stored.

Robin

Robins are considered a sign of spring, but they often overwinter in areas we think they've migrated away from.

When hunting for food, robins carefully watch for slight movements in the ground that can betray an earthworm close to the surface. Although we think of robins as living on worms, berries make up a larger portion of their diet.

Robin chicks have very few feathers when born, and their bulging eyes are closed for the first few days. Some winter roosts have as many as a quarter of a million robins in them.

Mourning Dove

Mourning doves can fly as fast as 60 miles per hour, although they generally travel at 30 to 40 mph.

The song of the mourning dove is often mistaken for an owl.

Mourning doves have a crop in their throats, a pouch for storing gathered seed until it can be digested.

Both male and female mourning doves produce crop milk, which is more solid than milk from mammals. High in protein and fat, crop milk is fed to baby birds.

Garden Slug

Slugs are hermaphrodites, which means that a slug possesses both male and female organs.

Each slug has two pairs of feelers—an upper set for seeing and a lower one for smelling and tasting. All feelers can be retracted and will grow back if lost.

Slugs secrete a layer of mucus, on which they travel; this prevents damage to the soft tissue of their foot. They can even travel over broken glass without injury.

They spend the winter in soil and can live for many years. Their eggs can stay inactive in the soil until conditions are right for them to hatch.

Honeybee

A bee needs to visit 4,000 flowers to gather enough nectar to make a single tablespoon of honey.

A beehive in summer can be home to as many as 80,000 bees.

In a beehive, one bee is chosen to be the queen and is fed a diet of royal jelly, a mix of pollen and a chemical produced by other bees. A queen can live for 3 to 5 years. The queen lays up to 2,000 eggs per day. Female worker bees can live 4 to 9 months in the winter but only for about 6 weeks in the summer. Male drones are only around during the summer and are expelled from the hive in the autumn.

Bees will only sting if provoked or protecting their hive. They can only sting once, since they die after stinging.

Bees are important to farmers because they pollinate crops. People also use the honey that bees make; use beeswax in candles, furniture polish, cosmetics, drugs, and art supplies; and use bee venom as a drug for treating arthritis and high blood pressure.

Ants

An ant can lift 20 times its weight. If you weighed 50 pounds and were as strong as an ant, you'd be able to lift 1,000 pounds!

A group of ants living together is called a colony. Each colony has a unique smell, so ants from other colonies are recognized immediately.

When an ant finds a food source, it leaves a trail that others in the colony can smell to help them find the food, too.

A colony can have one or more queens. The job of the queen ant is to lay eggs. Most ants live 45 to 60 days, but a queen can live many years. After a queen dies, the colony will survive only for a few months.

Caterpillar

Some caterpillars look like bird droppings or parts of the plants on which they feed; this bit of camouflage helps them survive to adulthood.

A caterpillar has 4,000 muscles, whereas a person has fewer than 700.

Most caterpillars are plant eaters, or herbivores, although some do eat other insects. Many caterpillars eat plants that have poisons that don't affect them but will affect animals that prey on them. These chemicals are also present in their adult stage.

A moth caterpillar spins a thick silk web called a cocoon; a butterfly caterpillar makes a smooth hard case called a chrysalis.

Cabbage White Butterfly

To tell the difference between male and female cabbage white butterflies, count the black spots on their top wings—the male has one on each; the female has two.

Cabbage white butterflies are often mistaken for moths, but like all butterflies (and unlike all moths), they have clubs on the tips of their antennae.

Every butterfly you see has been through four different stages in its life: egg, caterpillar (also called pupa), chrysalis, and finally, adult. (There are no baby butterflies—all butterflies are adults.)

Butterflies generally lay their eggs on only one type of plant, usually the type the caterpillars will eat. This is called the host plant; different species of butterflies have different host plants.

Ladybug

Farmers and gardeners are happy to see ladybugs in their fields, because the ladybugs eat small insects called aphids that suck the juices out of plants, which makes the plants die.

There are males, but they are also called ladybugs.

Ladybugs protect themselves by playing dead and releasing a small amount of bad-smelling blood from their legs, causing the predator to move along to a more lively lunch.

Ladybugs look for someplace warm to spend the winter and often end up in people's houses. They release chemicals called pheromones that can attract other ladybugs up to a quarter-mile away, so hundreds of ladybugs can congregate in the same place.

Praying Mantis

In French folklore, the praying mantis can guide a lost child home.

The praying mantis has excellent eyesight and can see up to 60 feet away.

There are 2,000 species of praying mantids; most are found in Asia. About 20 species are found in the US.

The praying mantis is the official state insect of Connecticut.

Housefly

The fly is the only flying insect with two wings—all others have four. A housefly's wings beat 200 times per second.

Houseflies feed on decaying food, feces (like dog poop), and the flesh of dead animals. They can only take in liquid, so must spit on their food to liquefy it in order to suck it back up. That's what they're doing when they land on your food. That and pooping. Think about that the next time a housefly lands on your ice cream cone!

Houseflies are found all over the world and have been known to carry over 100 diseases, such as typhoid, cholera, viral hepatitis, and salmonella.

The housefly goes through a complete metamorphosis: egg, larva (also called maggot), pupa, and adult. The adult lives about three weeks.

Spider

Spider webs are rich in vitamin K, which helps blood to clot, and can be used on wounds and cuts to staunch bleeding. There are 3,400 species of spiders in the US and Canada.

Some spiders eat yesterday's web and build a new one each day.

Spiders that spin webs in a spiral design are called orb weavers. Other spiders build funnel webs and wait inside for the vibrations that let them know an insect is on their web, then rush out to capture it. Still other spiders do not build webs at all, but leap upon their prey suddenly. A spider eats up to 2,000 insects per year.

Scientists organize living creatures by their similarities. They divide the entire animal kingdom into vertebrates (creatures with skeletons inside their bodies) and invertebrates (those with skeletons outside their bodies—called exoskeletons). One group of invertebrates is the arthropods—animals with exoskeletons, segmented bodies, and appendages that have joints. This includes spiders, insects, and crustaceans such as crabs, lobsters, and shrimp. Within that is the class Arachnida, which includes spiders, mites, ticks, and scorpions, and then the order Aranea, which is just spiders.

Squirrel

A squirrel will crack open a nut and rub it on its face before burying it. This will leave a scent on the nut that will help the squirrel find it later.

Because of how its eyes are positioned on its head, a squirrel can see some things behind it but can't see right in front of its nose.

A squirrel's four front teeth never stop growing, but they stay short because of all the gnawing the squirrel does.

Half of a squirrel's length is tail. It uses its tail for balancing, as shade from the hot sun, as shelter in the rain, for warmth in the winter, and as a means of communication with other squirrels.

Skunk

The spray from a skunk can cause temporary blindness. The great horned owl, which, like most birds, has a poor sense of smell, is the skunk's only serious predator.

Skunks are very accurate when spraying their foul-smelling scent. They can spray up to 10 feet away, and people can detect the odor as much as a mile away if they are downwind of it.

Skunks are crepuscular, which means they are most active at dawn and sunset.

Cricket

Crickets only chirp their songs when the temperature is above 52 degrees Fahrenheit. If you count the number of chirps in 15 seconds and add 40, you will know the outside temperature.

The male cricket chirps to attract female crickets and drive other males away. It rubs its left wing over its right, which has a ridged edge, to make the sound.

Most crickets are nocturnal, meaning they are more active at night than during the day.

In some countries, a cricket in the house is considered good luck, and people keep them as pets.

A Peek into the Poet's Toolkit

How do poets make poems? Some of the tools they use are rhyme, stanzas, meter, and poetic license.

RHYME

We all learn to recognize rhyming words when we're young—words that have the same vowel and consonant ending sound even though, as we learn later, they might be spelled differently—like chair, share, they're, and where.

Poets often use rhyming words at the ends of a poem's lines, and these are called end rhymes. Here's an example:

When warmer days begin to dawn
the robins come back to our lawn.

Sometimes poets use internal rhymes, too. This is when a word in the middle of a line rhymes with the last word.

Do you get a bit excited
when you spy a bird nearby?
Do you want to know some things
about some things that crawl or fly?

Here the rhyme we notice most is the end rhyme—nearby and fly—but there's also that word "spy" in the second line that adds to the poetry of the line without calling as much attention to itself.

When two lines in a row rhyme, that's called a rhyming couplet, as in the first example above. But not all poems are written in rhyming couplets.

STANZAS

Sometimes the poet breaks the poem into groups of lines called *stanzas*. (The word stanza comes from the Italian language and means room. You might imagine that a poem is a house with several rooms in it when you see a poem with stanzas.) A poet can break a poem into stanzas with the same or different numbers of lines or leave it as one long poem, depending on how he or she wants to organize the poem and how she wants it to look on the page. It's pretty much up to the poet, although there are some poetry forms that require stanzas of specified length.

In the second example above, there are four lines in the stanza, but only two of them rhyme. This has an A B C B rhyme scheme. That means that the second and fourth lines (the B lines) rhyme but the first and third lines (the A and C lines) don't.

Most of the poems in *Common Critters* have rhyming couplets, but a few have the A B C B rhyme scheme. There are other rhyme schemes used by poets (like A B C D E C, for instance), but there are no examples of them in this book.

METER

To understand meter, you have to understand that words are made up of syllables and that certain syllables are accented or stressed (pronounced harder than surrounding syllables). For example, the word "crow" has just one syllable, whereas the word "murder" has two syllables, the first of which is stressed or accented.

Poets use the number of syllables and those stressed syllables (also called beats) very carefully in the lines of their poems. Read this example out loud and notice how every other syllable is stressed, and there are four stressed syllables (or four beats) in each line:

Oh, shiny-black and noisy crow,
you are the loudest bird I know,

gathered with your friends in trees,
cawing harshly on the breeze.

Other poems might have two or three unstressed syllables before a stressed one. Look at the beginning of "Spider"; notice that each line has two unstressed syllables, then a stressed, then three unstressed, then a stressed, and each line has only two beats.

If you want to be a spider
here is what you need to do:
change the legs that you are wearing—
you'll need eight now, not just two—

You might think of this as:

ba-ba-BUM-ba-ba-ba-BUM-ba
ba-ba-BUM-ba-ba-ba-BUM
ba-ba-BUM-ba–ba-ba-BUM-ba
ba-ba-BUM-ba-ba-ba-BUM

Try tapping it out—tap one finger on the table for the ba syllable and tap your foot on the floor for the BUM syllable. Now read the lines again; do you hear the beats clearly in your head?

POETIC LICENSE

Just as artists get to exercise artistic license—exaggerating some features and eliminating others to achieve an effect—poets get to play with words and lines, making up some things and playing around with other things. This is called *poetic license*, naturally, and it's just one more form of *creative license*. Two lines in "Crow" are:

And could this fact be much absurder?
A group of you is called a murder!

"Absurder" is not a real word—the comparative form of "absurd" is "more absurd." But since adding the suffix "er" to an adjective is usually how the comparative is formed, readers will understand that the poet means "more absurd," and it adds a bit of humor to the poem by making it rhyme with murder.

Most poems don't change meter halfway through—if there are three beats to the line at the start of the poem, it usually ends with three beats to the line as well. "Earthworm," however, starts off with four beats per line for the first four-line stanza, then comes a stanza with only one word—but.

That one-word stanza signals a change, and the next stanza consists of four lines with only two beats each. Since that stanza is about the worm avoiding being eaten by birds, the change in the beat quickens the pace and gives a sense of the worm squirming quickly into a safe place to avoid a deadly encounter.

IN CONCLUSION

A poet makes many choices—what words to use, whether to rhyme or not, how many lines or stanzas a poem should have. The poet can make up words, can make up forms, can write in first, second, or third person, and can write about anything in or out of the entire world.

Poems can inform, entertain, express emotions, and share ideas. Writing poetry is a craft that poets get better at the harder and longer they work at it. If you would like to be a poet, now would be a great time to get started!